A Dishwasher's Handbook

Bobby Simonds

Copyright © 2020 Bobby Simonds

All rights reserved. No part of this publication may be reproduced, distributed, or transmitted in any form or by any means, including photocopying, recording, or other electronic or mechanical methods, without the prior written permission of the publisher, and/or author, except in the case of brief quotations embodied in critical reviews and certain other noncommercial uses permitted by copyright law. For permission requests, email **bobby.simonds@gmail.com** . Serious inquiries only.

https://bobbysimonds.com/

ISBN: **9798618975735**

ISBN 13: **XXXXX**

Library of Congress Control Number: **XXXXX**

LCCN Imprint Name: **Independently published**

https://www.amazon.com/bobbysimonds

Front Cover & Editing by author.

bobby.simonds@gmail.com

www.facebook.com/bobbyraysimonds

www.facebook.com/bobbyrsimonds

www.instagram.com/@bobbysimonds

#bobbysimonds

#BOBBYRAYSIMONDS

#ATWISTINTRAVEL

#risenfromtheashes

#toxicamerica

#Challenge-thyself

#avoidinghavoc

#bobbyscreativephotographyseries

#QUESTIONINGREALITY

#thedoctorscall

#evilmatters

#pandorasbox

#everythingchangeswithbrainsurgery

#UnfoldingMisery

#therealjerrylewis

#adishwashershandbook

From the Author:

I want to thank you ahead of time for your interest in this book, and others that you may read/purchase. Please be kind, and leave me a review after you finish, this book.

About the author:

As a self-taught author, I spend much time researching many various topics. This could very well include current events, current conspiracies, and current conspiracy gossip (which I put a spin on that name).

Between using Google & Youtube; one could easily lose themselves in this long, and eventful lavish web.

I have created/published many books; which with my nonfiction, I have more than enough proof, which I can not only keep up with current events, but years later, my books seem to stay up-to-date.

Like many authors before me, I too, am exceptionally observant. I am also intrigued with the successful, mindset of being an international author, and as I continue to write, my books become more successful because of people like you, who took a chance on something new, and original to read!

I was born with Mild Cerebral Palsy, and have had brain surgery. Which, I do not allow either to slow me down, and/or get in my way. I do not compare myself to other authors, however, I do believe I have what it takes.

Booklovers connect with me from my own personal biography. Connecting with readers on more of an emotional level; I decided to include topics such as: inner healing, conspiracy, grievance, political, suicide, & finishing up with positive outcomes.

On a side note, I have assisted others to glorify their dream, by directing them with the essentials for writing, and the publishing tools, that they would need, of course.

I've soared over topics such as, social media, "fake news," UFOs, the Alien Conspiracy, "mythical" creatures, religion, politics, cloning, life-sucking tablets. Furthermore, in one book, I even predicted Donald Trumps' win, before he was even close to upsetting Hilary Clinton's supporters.

As far as my fiction books go, I must say that I am still in the process of enjoying a world to create for my readers to escape their normal bubble, to enjoy somebody else's insanity. I currently only have one true novel, and the rest being, labeled as 'novella's' or short stories. Majority of my books, both fiction & nonfiction, generally are series. Obviously, I wrote a few individuals, but I prefer the other choice.

I hope that you are brave enough to leave your review of what you had thought of with this book, and others. Whether you are a previous supporter of mine, or a new one, be respectful and leave a review where you had purchased this book. Thanks for your participation, and I look forward to reading your review, or messages to me.
In addition, I hope you (the reader) check back on Amazon.com (or whatever link you purchased my titles), monthly, because I tend to publish a minimum of 5 books per year. Majority of the time, it's more realistically 10 books per year.

Half-Cocked

Today is your first day. You already have a background with cleaning dishes, from another restaurant or diner. You've even cleaned your own dishes from home. You believe that this job is merely a paycheck, and hey, it's just washing dishes!

The person who trains you, takes a measly 2 minutes to show you around, and teaches you incorrectly. Therefore, right off the get-co, you immediately have bad habits, because the trainer taught you incorrectly, or the sloppy-way, of doing things.

Because you are told, *you are the 'new' guy/gal*, you aren't sure how to handle this. Therefore, you keep this bad set of details to yourself for a bit.

Your supervisor is cool, open, and honest. He, or she, has an open-door policy. Meaning, share everything – good or bad, you witness.

By your second week, you've proven yourself, because of kicking-ass on the job. You are doing your job so well, that you receive compliments left and right. However, you still see the other dishwashers doing their jobs incorrectly, or half-cocked.

You feel brave enough to speak to the management team about the issues. You walk in the office, have a chat; then later, they have a chat with the staff. It appears, at first, it works for the first five minutes, then that supervisor leaves, and everything goes back to the way it was.

Knowing that there is always room for improvements, you read this book, and learn why it is important that ***Rules aren't always meant to be broken!***

Because the fact of the matter is, at any given job, that has to do with dishwashing, there really isn't room for errors. People can get sick, and often times, it's either the food or the dishes.

The Facts & Policies

This image is a Professional Dishwasher

Machine. The following, is the description:

Boost productivity and efficiency in your dish room with this CMA EST-66 high temperature conveyor dishwasher!

Designed for high-output applications, this dish machine moves racks of soiled dishware and glassware left to right along a conveyor, and utilizes two wash stages, a power heated rinse, and final rinse stages to ensure clean results. This system lets it handle up to 243 racks per hour, while using only 0.49 gallons of water per rack. An auto start / stop feature takes all the guesswork out of operation, and it also boasts an automatic soil purging system that filters debris into a removable, external tray.

Okay, with that out of the way, you can plainly see, you get what you pay for, right? This is the easiest part with working in a professional, dishwashing setting. The other side of the room, is for a three-bay sink, which this is where my concerns are. The reason, is because nobody seems to care about the health causing concerns are. Even though, they've experienced these symptoms before – yet they blame it on the cooking, not the cleaning of the dishes!

This seems self-explanatory, right?

The order of the images can be left to right, right to left. Either way, there is ALWAYS a RINSE cycle.

What happens to somebody without the rinse cycle? Diarrhea, is number one. Let me show you a list:

What diseases can you get from dirty dishes?

Coli, salmonella, and listeria on kitchen items that are often used for food preparation or storage. Salmonella, listeria, and some types of E. coli are among the many causes of foodborne illnesses, which sicken about 48 million Americans a year, according to the U.S. Centers for Disease Control and Prevention.

The following 7 steps are what will allow the proper cleaning with a 3-bay basin (sink). They're simple, and reliable. They are, A MUST FOLLOW APPLICATION, THAT SHOULDN'T BE OVER-LOOKED!

Step 1: Pre-Scrape & Pre-Soak. *This is meant for pots, especially, if they are caked with crap that won't simply be sprayed off!*

Step 2: Wash. *Your first basin should be filled with hot water (at least 110 degrees). It should also be with detergent solution (a type of soap). If installed properly, you shouldn't need to add water – hot or cold. It is supposed to be hot! All hot water added is only adding to bubble making, it should automatically be around 110 degrees – in temperature. Otherwise add hot water, and test the water, if need be.*

Step 3: Rinse. *Rinse the washed dishes. Be sure all soap is rinsed off all dishes and/or utensils, and pots. This is generally accomplished in the middle basin (sink). You can either use a sprayer (hose), or fill the basin with fresh clean water, about half-way, and dip them.*

Step 4: Sanitize. Sanitize the rinsed items in the third basin (sink). The water should be hot water, or a chemical solution (which should also be hot, for best cleansing results). Do not rinse after sanitizing. And a big FYI, the sanitizer is PINK.

Step 5: Dry. Items must air dry on a clean, drainboard, or rack.

Step 6: Clean and sanitize working equipment.

Step 7: Check your water. *Your soaking sink and sanitizing sink should always appear clean.*

Obviously, your soaking basin will become dirty more frequently. Nonetheless, it should be refilled on an as-needed basis. Don't allow the temperature to drop, if not using frequently. If this occurs, drain the sink, clean excess food out, then refill it. This step is my personal, add-on.

If you must sanitize, using only hot water: Water <u>**MUST**</u> be at least <u>171 DEGREES</u>, and dishes must also be submerged for a minimum of <u>30 SECONDS</u>!

Furthermore, working equipment should be washed, and sanitized themselves, every 4 hours. This doesn't happen as often as you would think. Things can become quite hectic in a kitchen, and even during down-time, people don't feel up to doing these essentials – they'd rather socialize.

Proper Dishwashing Procedures
2 Compartment Sink Method

Kitchen Groups	Sink #1	Sink #2	Counter/Drying Rack
All groups must scrape their dishes of excess materials before handing to the dishwashers.	Dishes must be washed in *warm* soapy water (minimum 43'C/110'F). Always use clean water. Refill sink as necessary.	Warm water (not less than 24'C/75'F) For a minimum of 45 seconds + Bleach (100 PPM) OR Hot Water (77'C/170'F)	Air Dry And Store
Scrape and Pre-Rinse	**Wash and Rinse**	**Sanitize**	**Drying and Storage**

This is generally what we do at home, but I have seen in a smaller setting. It's common sense, however, nobody realizes how to use it anymore!

WASH RINSE SANITIZE: ULTIMATE GUIDE TO MANUAL WAREWASHING

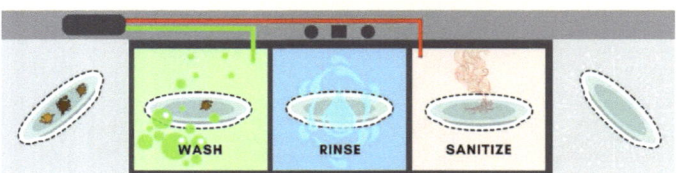

It seems easy, right?

Surprisingly, this is all basic knowledge, if you properly trained. Still, people get comfortable, and lazy. Some are simply lazy.

Don't become those people. Be strong. Put your best foot forward, and be the person you want to be. Stand up, and do your job. Work together, and force your team to do their part – it will take time, but repetition is key.

Another main issue with work, is not washing your hands enough. It amazes me how people walk around with bacteria on their hands, not caring about how it causes health issues. This is especially essential, in the food industry, more than other types of businesses!

One of the issues I've witnessed with many jobs (that I had in this industry, as a dishwasher), is that people will run the silverware thru the dishwashing machine. Collect the silverware in a silverware container, then walk over to the sanitizing sink, and dip the silverware in the water with sanitizer…Um, why?

These various types of people, claim it is because of their training.

Dishwasher's already have a bad rep for that part in the food industry. It's as though, they are viewed at the bottom of the food chain, the bad seeds – if you must.

Not all rules are meant to be broken; if you do your job right, all things will align! Furthermore, do it fast, do it accurately, and people could take you more seriously.

On a side note, be weary with lifting around 40 pounds (this is mainly lifting plates). Bending is a big part of the job, as is, pivoting & standing (in one place). If you have weak hands, also be advised [when using the hose/sprayer], that over long periods of time, your hands will swiftly weaken, and could cause pain.

Another, FYI... Be advised, even though you are a dishwasher, it can get severely hot in that department. Heat is the main source of your water, and dishwasher – plus the humidity that comes out of the machine. Therefore, if you suffer from migraines, be certain you take precautions, and always remember to always carry medication with you!

Tell your manager about this book, and advise them to purchase a copy for each member of your team. All pictures inside this book are up-to-date with the FDA, and HEALTH DEPARTMENTS. It doesn't change from state-to-state, it's all the same in America!

The Real Issue

The real issue is, working with slackers, is that they don't know why they are following the rules, set before them. They need to be forced to understand them, to follow them. And with others, they need to be fired for wrongful doings, with choosing not to follow them, simply because they don't care.

People that don't care about their job duties, take for granted with even having a job. Having a job is a privilege, that people don't realize. Kind of like having a driver's license. There are risks with having one, but it's up to you to decide to keep it.

Part 2:

Chapter 1

Being an overachiever, I pick up the slack, and feel overwhelmed with frustration, do you?

Every time I choose to work this type of job, my hands hurt like nothing I've ever experienced before; which makes typing, that much more difficult. My mind is blank most of the time, and I feel as though I have become a robot, day in, and day out.

I feel empty inside, and majority of that feeling, is due to not writing!

Chapter 2

People get comfortable. Whereas, I don't take my time doing things. Perhaps, it is due to being an overachiever, with creating such a vast collection of books, which of course, has brought me to be excellent with whatever I put my mind to. Obviously, my grammar isn't the greatest, but I make do, thanks to the basic's with using MS Word!

Don't get me wrong, this job position is tough, for anyone. I love the phrase, ***"Why wait for tomorrow, when you can do today."*** This quote applies to life, and work. Why wait to do something, when you have the time to do it now? Hence, why let yourself get further behind with work duties, if you have time standing around, watching the fastest guy on your team, do everything else, for you? Why not jump in and help? When did this become such a childish game?

Again, why wait until tomorrow? Do it now, this instance! [Or at least, after you finish reading this manual!]

Chapter 3

When running any business, it's difficult for the President of the company to find 'good help.' It's like the *Zip-Recruiter* commercials say, ***it's like finding a needle in a haystack!***

They're not joking.

When the good help arrives, the rest of the team looks like donkey-poo, and the 'new guy' turns out to be shovel. *Shoveling everybody's donkey-poo-poo!* I know, I'm arrogant. Nevertheless, when you self-train yourself on something [and everything], are motivated for a paycheck, and have been out of a slave-job for as long as I have, at many periods in my life, you know that you have no time to slack off. You give it your all, on any given day. Because, in the back of your mind, you know this job isn't meant for you, being a creative, intelligent writer. As a book title comes to mind, *"We're surrounded by stupids!"* (And I wrote it that way for a reason!) Because I truly believe, that people take life for granted, rolling with the flow is not my way of life, I enjoy standing out, good or bad. I know I am successful, and I also know I am intelligent, especially working in the food industry, as a *dishwasher*, just like you! I don't care if you are slower, but after two years, you should be able to keep a good flow in the kitchen. Otherwise, you should run for hills, because *Bobby's here! (LOL)*

Thanks for reading, and don't forget to leave a review where you purchased this copy, and others.

Be sure to visit my website, and/or Amazon.com/bobbysimonds

You've got to take the time to read other books I've created and provided for you – my audience – with over 70+ titles!

Furthermore, express to your supervisor with any questions or concerns with what may not be up to code – based on staff or equipment. Who knows, things could improve!